Essential Question...
How can learning about the past help you understand the present?

Treks Through Time

by **Ashleigh Thompson,**
Red Lake Band of Ojibwe

Introduction

Archaeology is the study of the past. It takes place all over the world in different environments.

Archaeologists often dig at a **site** for **evidence**. They remove earth to **reveal** what is underground. They look for **artifacts**. Archaeologists call the **objects** people used *artifacts*. We might call them *belongings*.

Archaeologists can work underground— or underwater!

Archaeology helps us learn about the way people lived. Archaeologists learn a lot by asking questions. For example, they might ask: *Did all adults wear jewelry?* Archaeology is important. It helps students learn about the past. It helps **descendant communities** (descendants of the people the archaeologist is studying) learn about their ancestors.

Chapter 1

The Beginning

Archaeology starts with a **research** question. Dr. Smith is a Native American archaeologist. She wants to know how the ancient Mississippian culture built mounds. They built them at a site called Cahokia. It is in Illinois. She begins by collecting information. She will read books about the Mississippian culture.

Dr. Smith will visit museums. She will study artifacts to help answer her research question.

Dr. Smith can also ask descendant communities for information. They may have an **oral tradition** and records.

If Dr. Smith needs more information she will excavate, or dig at the site. She will work with the people whose ancestors she will study.

There are many things Dr. Smith needs to do to get ready for this **expedition**.

To prepare, Dr. Smith must answer these questions. *How many people are needed? What tools will they need? How will they* **preserve** *the artifacts they find?* Deciding to excavate is a big decision. The land is never the same afterwards.

Cahokia, a Native American City

Cahokia is the site of an ancient city. It was built by Native peoples. They lived there from AD 1050 to AD 1300. The Native Americans used complex planning to build the city. Cahokia once had over 100 human-made earthen mounds. Today, there are only 80 mounds. The largest is called Monks Mound.

Monks Mound is as tall as a ten-story building. It is as long as three football fields.

A dig on the Mashantucket Pequot Reservation

Tribal Historic Preservation Office

In the United States, many Native American tribes have a special office. This office protects ancient sites. It works with archaeologists. The office makes sure artifacts and sacred objects are given back to the tribes. The Mille Lacs Band of Ojibwe in Minnesota has such an office. An archaeologist works in the office. He makes sure that important Ojibwe sites are not harmed.

STOP AND CHECK

What do archaeologists have to do before they can excavate a site?

Chapter 2

The Dig

Archaeologists have a special way to dig. Dr. Smith makes a grid on the ground. Then she labels each square of the grid. This helps her team know where each artifact comes from.

Dr. Smith's team removes buckets of dirt from their squares. They use shake screens with tiny holes to sift through the dirt. Small pieces of tools and pottery are left in the screens.

The team scrapes the bottom of their squares with shovels. They are looking for **features**. For example, an outline of charcoal means there is a fireplace there.

Archaeologists can use everyday objects to learn about the lives of ancient people.

A graduate student records information at a dig.

Teams **document** the artifacts they find. They note where the items were found and describe them.

As the team digs deeper, they **uncover** older things. An artifact found near the surface could be 300 years old. But an artifact found several feet deeper could be from an earlier **era**.

Archaeologists find more than artifacts at sites. Sometimes they find human remains. By testing bone and teeth samples, the team can discover if the person is male or female. They can also tell their age.

Dr. Smith must be careful if she finds human remains. They might come from the ancestors of descendant communities. The community may not want their ancestors moved. Sometimes, the community will allow the study of remains. Then the archaeologists work closely with the descendants.

Dr. Smith will take a sample of earth from the mound. The sample will have layers of soil. It will tell her how the mound was built and what it was made of.

STOP AND CHECK

Why does Dr. Smith take a sample of earth from the mound?

Chapter 3

More than a Dig

After the dig, artifacts will be safely stored and studied. Dr. Smith will learn a **tremendous** amount from the artifacts. Perhaps Dr. Smith's team found a hide scraper. This tool tells her that people at the site made clothes from animal hides.

The team will study what kind of stone was used to make the tool. What if the stone came from far away? Dr. Smith might decide that the Mississippian people traded with others who lived far away.

It is better to be safe than sorry! Some artifacts might break. They are stored in special bags and boxes so they are protected.

Radiocarbon dating can be used on bone, wood, plants, or anything else that was once alive.

Dr. Smith took charcoal samples from next to the mound. She can date the charcoal with radiocarbon dating. Things that were once alive have carbon. Carbon is not **permanent**. It decays over time. The amount of carbon left in an object tells her how old it is. Dr. Smith will measure the carbon in the charcoal. It will tell her how old it is and how old the mound is.

Places such as universities and museums store artifacts. Museum exhibits teach people about what archaeologists have learned.

However, descendant communities may want artifacts returned. In the United States, archaeologists are required by law to work with descendant communities.

Not all descendant communities want artifacts returned. Sometimes they only wish to visit objects that are **sacred** to them. Such artifacts are special. But they may also be seen and studied by everyone.

STOP AND CHECK

Why is it important for archaeologists to work with descendant communities?

The Heard Museum of American Indian Art and History is in Phoenix, Arizona. It displays art and artifacts.

Conclusion

In the past, archaeologists could do what they wanted with artifacts. Little respect was paid to Native American lands and artifacts. Today's laws make sure archaeologists in the United States work with descendant communities.

Archaeology is a team effort. Archaeologists work with a team when they excavate. They ask other scientists questions. They work with and learn from descendant communities. The future of archaeology is bright. There are many more ways to learn about the past.

Excavating is one way that archaeologists learn about the past.

Summarize

Use details from *Treks Through Time* to summarize the selection. Your graphic organizer may help you.

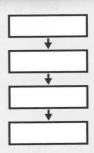

Text Evidence

1. Use the information on pages 4-5 to explain the steps archaeologists follow before they decide to dig. SEQUENCE

2. Find the word *excavate* on page 4. What does it mean? What clues in the text helped you figure it out? VOCABULARY

3. Write about how today's archaeologists work with descendant communities. Use details from the text in your answer. WRITE ABOUT READING

Compare Texts

Read about a conflict between archaeologists and a descendant community over a very important find.

The Ancient One

The Ancient One lived over 8000 years ago. He is also called Kennewick Man. His bones were found in 1996 near Kennewick, Washington in the Columbia River.

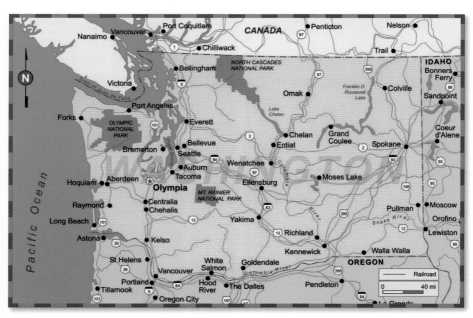

The Kennewick Man is now at the Burke Museum in Seattle, Washington.

Facial reconstruction helps us understand what the person may have looked like.

After the Ancient One was found, the Confederated Tribes of the Umatilla Indian Reservation wanted to rebury him. The Umatilla's oral history says the Ancient One is part of their tribe. A group of scientists disagreed. They said that the Ancient One was not Native American. Other scientists agreed that the Ancient One was Native American. But they wanted the right to study the skeleton. The scientists sued the government. They did not want the Ancient One returned to the Umatilla. The case took nine years. The Umatilla lost the case. The court said the Ancient One was not related to living Native Americans.

Scientists continue to study the Ancient One. In 2015, Danish scientists tested his DNA. They found that the Ancient One is closely related to Native Americans. The Umatilla hopes this new research will help them reclaim the Ancient One.

This conflict is an example of what can happen when people have different beliefs about their ancestors. Laws were made to help tribes **repatriate** (get back from museums or other institutions) their sacred objects and the remains of their people.

Make Connections

Why did the Danish scientists' findings in 2015 give new hope to the Umatilla? ESSENTIAL QUESTION

What steps do you think scientists followed when collecting and studying the remains of the Ancient One? TEXT TO TEXT

Glossary

artifacts *(AHR-ti-fakts)* objects that are made by human beings *(page 2)*

features *(FEE-churz)* parts of a site that were created and used by people, such as a grave or fire pit *(page 7)*

oral tradition *(OHR-uhl truh-DISH-uhn)* a community's culture and history that is carefully memorized and preserved by word of mouth from person to person *(page 4)*

preserve *(pri-ZURV)* to make something last *(page 5)*

repatriate *(ree-PAT-ree-ayt)* to return something to its nation of origin *(page 18)*

Index

Focus on
Social Studies

Purpose To understand the connections between the past and the present

Procedure

Step 1 ▶ Choose an everyday object that many people use, such as a cup, a jacket, or a phone.

Step 2 ▶ Carry out some research to find out what people would have used in the past instead of the object.

Step 3 ▶ Try to imagine what people in the future might use instead of the object. What would it look like? How would it work?

Step 4 ▶ Make a timeline and illustrate how your object changes over time, from the past, to the present day, and into the future.